TEACHINGS ON HEAVEN

By

John Yates

All royalties from this book will be donated to The Falls Church Anglican. The amazing story of this church is told in *The Awakening of Washington's Church*, by J.B. Simmons.

Copyright © John Yates 2018
All right reserved.

Cover design by Jessica Blanchard.

ISBN: 978-1986397544

Printed in the United States of America

CONTENTS

Foreword

Chapter 1
Looking Forward to Heaven? 1

Chapter 2
Heaven *Now* Is Not Heaven *Forever* 14

Chapter 3
What Is Life Like In Heaven *Now*? 33

FOREWORD

Heaven must be indescribably wonderful since it is God's eternal home! The fact that he desires our presence there with him is beyond imagining. Over the years I have read everything I could find to help me better envision our future home. These three teachings are aimed at answering some of our questions and raising more for your contemplation. I have read many good books about Heaven but none as helpful personally as Randy Alcorn's encyclopedic study – *Heaven*.

I hope this will stimulate you to pay close attention to what scripture tells us about New Heaven and New Earth and that you will let your imagination "take off" as you do.

John Yates

Chapter 1

Looking Forward to Heaven?

During the final year before my mother died, I periodically talked with her about heaven. She had a robust faith and a certainty about heaven based upon the promises of scripture. She believed deeply that heaven is a gift offered, not to those who <u>deserve</u> it, but to those who come to God in humble, repentant faith in Jesus Christ. Towards the end she said that she wasn't thinking a great deal about the next life, said she wasn't "homesick for heaven" yet, but would be ready for the journey whenever the time came. I realized that even during her final days, she was concentrating on the now, the people who were with her at the moment – she wanted very much to live in the present, which is a good thing.

Many believers, however, are not comfortable <u>ever</u> thinking or talking about the next life because they fear it.

They trust that their sins have been forgiven through Christ, they trust that God _has_ promised them eternal life, and they are profoundly grateful . . . but they just don't like to think about it. What was it Woody Allen said – "I don't mind the idea of dying, I just don't want to be there when it happens." I'm sure _some_ believers _do_ harbor those secret apprehensions, but what I encounter more is, sadly, _misconceptions_ about heaven that cause us to avoid the topic.

One pastor confessed to a friend, "Whenever I think about heaven, it makes me depressed. I'd rather just cease to exist when I die." "Why?" his friend asked. "I can't stand the thought of that endless tedium. To float around in the clouds with nothing to do but strum a harp...it's all so terribly boring. Heaven doesn't sound much better than hell. I'd rather be annihilated than spend eternity in a place like that."

Sadly, many ministers who ought to know better share this joyless view of heaven. When an English vicar was asked by a colleague what he expected after death, he replied, "Well, if it comes to that, I suppose I shall enter into eternal bliss, but I really wish you wouldn't bring up such depressing subjects."

Let me be personal. For most of my life, whenever the idea of heaven and eternal life came into my mind, I'd usually push it aside – not because I was afraid, but I think it was because I had huge misconceptions about heaven, and so many questions to which there appeared to be no answer. St. Paul said that to die and depart and be with Christ is far, far better than staying on a sin-marred, sin-cursed earth. But I found it hard to grasp.

During one significant three year period in my life I felt driven to face up to this and focused much of my Bible reading and study time on this very subject. It was just fantastic! My whole thinking about heaven changed because I began to ask just what does the Bible tell us, and as I've contemplated all it says, I've begun to use my imagination. The result is I am anticipating heaven with joy and gladness and excitement I never thought possible. And I want to ask, are you?

C.S. Lewis said:

> Most of us find it very difficult to want "heaven" at all – except in so far as "heaven" means meeting again our friends who have died. One reason for this difficulty is that we have not been trained: our whole education tends to fix our minds on this world. Another reason is that when the real want for heaven is present in us, we do not recognize it.

Heaven will be, for followers of Christ, the realization of our deepest longings – the fulfillment beyond our greatest hopes. Charles Spurgeon said about this:

> To come to Thee is to come home from exile, to come to land out of the raging storm, to come to rest after long labor, to come to the goal of my desires and the summit of my wishes.

The early Christians had such a powerful vision of life after death! One historian writes that drawings on the catacomb walls, left by believers who died during the early Roman persecution, picture heaven with beautiful landscapes, children playing, and people feasting at banquets. These tombs where martyrs were buried are inscribed with statements like: "He was taken up into his eternal home!" or "In Christ, Alexander is not dead but lives."

About 125 A.D., a Greek named Aristides wrote to a friend about Christianity, trying to explain why this new faith was growing so rapidly. "If any righteous man among the Christians passes from this world, they rejoice and offer thanks to God, and they escort his body with songs and thanksgiving as if he were setting out from one place to another nearby."

In the third century, the church father Cyprian said about death:

> Let us greet the day which assigns each of us to his own home, which snatches us from this place and sets us free from the snares of the world, and restores us to paradise and the kingdom. Anyone who has been in foreign lands longs to return to his own native land. . . We regard paradise as our native land.

Paul wrote to the Corinthians:

As long as we are at home in the body we are away from the Lord... We... would prefer to be away from the body and at

home with the Lord." (2 Corinthians 5: 6, 8)

Many believers have lost this sense of eagerness about heaven because we have simply lost sight of heaven. The church hasn't taught about heaven very much – perhaps because we don't want to be accused of being too focused on the next life, afraid of being "so heavenly minded, we'll be of no earthly good." Many of the great theologians have steered away from the topic. John Calvin hardly dealt with it at all. Louis Berkof, who I studied in seminary and who wrote so thoroughly about faith, only devotes one page to heaven in his classic, Systematic Theology. Reinhold Neibuhr's influential two volume text titled, The Nature and Destiny of Man, says nothing at all about heaven.

In scripture, eternity is the crucial, fixed point of reference, like the North Star is to the sailor.

The certainty of judgment, the fear of hell, the longing for heaven, are essential to a biblical world view, but Moderns just don't like to think about these things, and when folks nowadays do think about heaven, it's usually a mishmash of ideas culled from television, the media, different religions. People have a highly subjective view, partly because they don't know what the scriptures say, and partly this is because of Satan. Jesus told us the devil is the father of lies, and some of his biggest and best lies are about heaven – he doesn't want God's people to know about God's home. He is described in Revelation 13:6 as opening "his mouth to blaspheme God and God's dwelling place and those who dwell in heaven." He despises God's person and God's people and God's place – heaven – because he was kicked out of heaven when he rebelled against God. (Isaiah 14:12-15) And so, our enemy has sown seeds of untruth about the next life.

In one of John Eldredge's books, The Journey of Desire, he writes:

> Nearly every Christian I have spoken with has some idea that eternity is an unending church service . . . We have settled on an image of the never-ending sing-along in the sky, one great hymn after another, forever and ever, amen. And our heart sinks. Forever and ever? That's it? That's the good news? And then we sigh and feel guilty that we are not more "spiritual." We lose heart, and we turn once more to the present to find what life we can.

The two reasons we worry we won't be happy in heaven are that we don't know what the Bible tells us about it, and we fail to use our imagination when we do read what scripture says about it. Heaven will not be dreary and boring. We won't find ourselves wishing we'd brought along a magazine! We won't float around in disembodied existence, and we won't wish for eternity to end. Those who are in heaven will not long for anything more. The biblical images of heaven are images of intense delight, matchless beauty, glorious music, banqueting, learning, belonging, loving, serving, laughing. Images of gardens, cities, forests, rivers, kingdoms, exploration. It is a place where people with real bodies are experiencing the fulfillment of their every good desire. One of the most important pictures of heaven is gleaned from the words of Jesus in John 14, where he describes heaven as home:

> **Don't let this throw you. You trust God, don't you? Trust me. There is plenty of room for you in my Father's home. If that weren't so, would I have told you that I'm on my way to get a room ready for you? And if I'm on my way to get your room ready, I'll come back and get you so you can live where I live. (Petersen's <u>The Message</u>)**

Here is one of the most wonderful, amazing passages in all the Bible. I'd like you to think closely about what Jesus said, and then let your imagination take over.

There are <u>three absolutes</u> in these words of Jesus. First, he speaks with <u>absolute certainty</u>:

> **What I am telling you is absolutely true! You do not have to be wondering or worrying about this. You have learned to trust me. Now just keep doing so.**

Jesus had told his friends that his time was short, that he'd be betrayed, arrested, and executed. They were confused, sad, perplexed, ashamed, because he had just spoken to them about their pride, and they were wavering in their faith! (How could someone who's about to be executed be the Messiah?) But Jesus asked them to trust him. "You trust God – well, trust me, too, because I am right in the center of my father's will. What I am about to tell you is absolutely true."

Second, he is speaking of <u>absolute reality</u>. In 14:2:

> **In my Father's house there are many dwelling-places. If it were not so, would I have told you that I go to prepare a place for you?**

Jesus is describing heaven: heaven is where God is (Our Father, who art in heaven). Heaven is described as <u>home</u> – my father's house – singular – it is God's own personal dwelling place – it is permanent, it is solid, it is a <u>place</u>.

Skip Ryan, known to many of you, says this:

> All of the Bible's images of our future in heaven, including this one, are concrete. <u>We</u> think of heaven as abstract, ghostlike, somehow <u>less real</u> than this existence. But the Bible presents heaven as a place more real than this existence, a place where the senses are more attuned, more alive to the taste of the finest wine, the aroma of the feast, the sound of a thousand choirs, the sight of a million angels.

What we don't understand is that heaven is <u>more</u> real than earth. We think of <u>this</u> life as concrete, real, but here we only see and perceive a portion of reality. In his wonderful book, <u>The Great Divorce</u>, C.S. Lewis attempts to help us see this. Lewis takes us on an imaginary bus trip to heaven with a group of prim and proper English tourists. The minute they get off the bus in heaven for their brief, temporary tour, they appear ghost-like. Lewis describes them as transparent compared to everything else in heaven, which is solid and real. The visitors from London take off their shoes to go walking on the pretty green grass in the park, but the grass is so real and so strong that it hurts their tender, ghostlike feet. He calls the people who dwell in heaven 'solid people,' and the earthlings are the 'ghosts'. What Lewis is teaching is that heaven is <u>more real than earth</u>.

Can we possibly even <u>begin</u> to imagine what a home, fit for God to dwell in, would be like? How beautiful must it be! How spacious! How comfortable! How pleasing! How amply provided! Some of us enjoy roominess, spaciousness. It will be spacious! Some of us enjoy coziness. It will be intimate. It will be <u>absolutely appropriate</u> (the third absolute). In John 14:2b-3:

> **In my Father's house there are many dwelling-places. If it were not so, would I have told you that I go to prepare a place for you? And if I go and prepare a place for you, I will come again and will take you to myself, so that where I am, there you may be also.**

Jesus went through the cross and grave and resurrection in order to open the way for us to the place he called home. He told his disciples that he would be <u>readying</u> it for all those who follow him in faith. The image is of a parent, preparing his child's room just especially for the child. When you have a son or daughter and you have the means to give them a room of their own, you want it to be just right. I've noticed that when parents are moving in or decorating their home, usually the last room they focus on is their <u>own</u> bedroom – it's typically still in need of paint and wallpaper, long after they've moved in because they've given their attention to the rooms where the ones they love will be living. You want it to be <u>right</u>, with curtains and bed covers, with bookshelves and rugs that are just right. A place for a dollhouse, a box for the toys, a storage bin for baseball gloves and games, a special shelf for that child's special collection.

If the master carpenter of Nazareth is preparing a place for one he loves, it will be perfect – it will be home. There is no place like home! My wife, Susan and I were picking up around the house the other day, putting together some flower arrangements, and she said, "Oh, I just love our house!" One of my children was here this week and she said, "Dad, I just love to come home – it's so happy here – there is no place like it." Home, for the blessed and fortunate person, is memories of family and childhood, meals and parties, pets, friends over the years; it's the feel of the bed, the old, familiar fragrance when you come in the door, the books in the den, the furniture you've rested on so many times, the old quilt hanging on the rack, the family portraits – it's just home. Home is where we retreat to be alone, to enjoy those we love, and to welcome our guests. It is uniquely ours. Take all the good and happy memories and feelings you have ever had about a home place, and then you have just the barest beginning of what our heavenly home will be like – it will be <u>our own</u> – just right for you and your loved ones. And it will be with the Lord – "I will take you to myself so that where I am, there you may be also."

God is with us now, in the person of the Holy Spirit, who indwells each believer. But we can't see or touch him. In heaven Christ will be our ever present companion. He will be in the midst of all his people and we will no longer be separated from the Father or the Son. We will share in that unspeakable union where, in Paul's words, **we shall always be with the Lord. (1 Thessalonians 4:17)**

I'd like to whet your appetite for more as I lay out some of the things I hope to explain. Heaven is not far away. It is near, near enough to see into for those to whom it is given. At the end of time, this earth will be changed; it will be redeemed. Heaven will come down. There will be a New Earth and a New Heaven. This world, amplified, purified, expanded, fulfilled, will be joined to heaven. Earth will be familiar yet wonderfully different. Those in heaven now are in a different state than they will be after the establishment of the New

Heaven and New Earth. Our bodies will be changed in heaven but we will eat, drink, laugh and play, work, study, serve, explore. There will be a sense of time passing but no sense of longing for an end to come. Time will be different. We will be closer to those we love than we can imagine. Love will be richer, deeper, perfected. We will understand one another, fully. Our ethnic distinctions and cultural distinctions likely will all still be apparent, but there will be a unity of purpose we simply do not know here. Animals – wild, domestic – will be there. Perhaps we will converse with them! We will entertain in our home, join in cultivating the garden of paradise. Our home will be in a great, eternal city whose splendor and dimensions are so great, so lovely. We will build on what in this life was just begun: musicians' and artists' creativity will be perfected; builders will build majestically; storytellers will entertain; your favorite sport in heaven may be one you don't even know here. <u>However</u> God has wired you here on earth, in heaven your wiring will be perfected, your achievement beyond imagining. Joy, as Lewis said, will be the business of heaven. The sick will be gloriously well. The blind will see with perfect clarity. The mute, the lame, the paralyzed, the weak, the deaf – all will enjoy complete, vital health.

Perhaps Victor Hugo described it as well as any:

> I feel within me that future life. I am like a forest that has been razed; the new shoots are stronger and brighter. I shall most certainly rise toward the heavens the nearer my

approach to the end, the plainer is the sound of immortal symphonies of worlds which invite me. For half a century I have been translating my thoughts into prose and verse: history, drama, philosophy, romance, tradition, satire, ode, and song; all of these I have tried. But I feel I haven't given utterance to the thousandth part of what lies within me. When I go to the grave I can say, as others have said, "My day's work is done." But I cannot say, "My life is done." My work will recommence the next morning. The tomb is not a blind ally; it is a thoroughfare. It closes upon the twilight, but opens upon the dawn.

Chapter 2

Heaven *Now* Is Not Heaven *Forever*

Thinking biblically about the next life energizes us for this life. Learning about heaven causes us to love earth more and more, contrary to what you might expect. And "setting our minds on things above," as Paul commanded the Colossians (3:1-4), helps us to become all the more committed to living by heaven's priorities, here, now. Let's revisit some common assumptions about heaven and recall what we actually know.

What We Assume About Heaven	What the Bible Says About Heaven
Non-Earth	New Earth
Unfamiliar; otherworldly	Familiar; earthly

What We Assume About Heaven	What the Bible Says About Heaven
Disembodied	Resurrected (embodied)
Foreign	Home (all the comforts of home with all the innovations of an infinitely creative God)
Leaving favorite things behind	Retaining the good; finding the best ahead
No time and space	Time and space
Static	Dynamic
Neither old (like Eden) nor new and earthly; just strange and unknown	Both old and new
Nothing to do; floating on the clouds	A God to worship and serve; a universe to rule; purposeful work to accomplish; friends to enjoy
No learning or discovery; instant and complete knowledge	An eternity of learning and discovering
Boring	Fascinating
Loss of desire	Continuous fulfillment of desire
Absence of the terrible (but presence of little we desire)	Presence of the wonderful (everything we desire and nothing we don't)

Let's back up a bit and ask, what happens when we die? And is there a <u>difference</u> in the heaven that deceased believers inhabit <u>now</u> and the New Heaven and the New Earth that is to come?

First, what happens at death? Maybe you have a collection of famous last words. I have some favorites:

- Dylan Thomas: "I've had 18 straight whiskies. I think that's the record."
- Oscar Wilde: "Either that wallpaper goes or I do."
- After sinking his final putt on a golf course, Bing Crosby said, "It was a great game." And then he collapsed.

Some, of course, are darker, sadder statements:

- Princess Diana, as recorded in the official police files of Paris, said, "My God. What's happened?"
- "Don't turn down the lights," said O'Henry, the famous story writer, "I'm afraid to go home in the dark."
- Mrs. John Connally, wife of the then governor of Texas, just prior to President Kennedy's fatal shooting, had exclaimed to the President, "Mr. President, you can't say that Dallas doesn't love you." To which Kennedy replied, "<u>That's</u> obvious."

We're always curious about a dying person's final words because we're always looking for more insight into what happens.

Scientists tell us that at the moment of death electrical activity in the brain ceases. Consciousness is thought to end, and the heart and lungs stop functioning. The body's metabolism ceases and soon the body begins to cool and become pallid. The muscles stiffen within a few hours and physical decay begins internally. One thing is quite certain, the body is dead. What happens to the spirit, however, is a question science cannot answer.

Jesus, at his death said, **Into thy hands I commit my spirit.**

Does the Bible tell us what happens at death? Well, yes and no – it doesn't answer many of our questions but it answers the most important ones about a person's destiny after death. That's what we want to consider today.

What the scriptures are clear about, is that after death comes judgment. **It is appointed for mortals to die once, and after that the judgment. (Hebrews 9:27)**

St. Paul summarized the whole of scripture on this: **We shall all stand before the judgment seat of God. (Romans 14:10)**

There is a sorting out, a final examination at which only the Lord is fit to preside – a moment when every human being will be judged. The various descriptions in the Bible about God's judgment have always been somewhat confusing to me, even though the main point is perfectly clear – my life, my deeds, my thoughts, my intentions, will be judged by our righteous, holy God.

What has helped me enormously has been to realize that there are two judgments that all who die will face – not just the great and final judgment at the end of time when Christ returns, but there is another prior to that.

The first judgment is the judgment pronounced upon our lives at the moment we die. It determines our immediate destiny and condition after death. It is based not on our deeds but on faith – whether or not we have trusted in Christ. What do I mean?

The New Testament teaches that we receive forgiveness from God, through faith in his Son in this life, forgiveness that saves us from ever being parted from God. We see this repeated <u>many</u> times in the Bible. John 3:16 comes to mind:

> **For God so loved the world that he gave his only Son, so that everyone who believes in him may not perish but may have eternal life. Indeed, God did not send the Son into the world to condemn the world, but in order that the world might be saved through him.**

And Ephesians 2:8-9:

> **For by grace you have been saved through faith, and this is not your own doing; it is the gift of God— not the result of works, so that no one may boast.**

But listen also to Jesus' amazing promise recorded in John 5:24:

> **Very truly, I tell you, anyone who hears my word and believes him who sent me has eternal life…has passed from death to life.**

In Titus 3:5-7, St. Paul wrote:

> **He saved us, not because of any works of righteousness that we had done, but according to his mercy, through the washing of rebirth and renewal by the Holy Spirit. This Spirit he poured out on us richly through Jesus Christ our Savior, so that, having been justified by his grace, we might become heirs according to the hope of eternal life.**

It's for this reason that St. Paul concludes at the end of Romans 8, that even in dying, the believer <u>cannot</u> be separated from God: **Nothing can ever separate the believer from him and his love – not even death.**

Jesus confirms this over and over again – that when we die a judgment is pronounced at that moment upon our life based upon our faith in him – he assumes this. For instance, in his parable of the rich man and Lazarus, as soon as death comes, the poor man of faith is gathered to God's presence – the rich man whose life exhibited no faith, is in the place of torment, in anguish.

Either we go to God **(Enter into the joy of the master,** says Jesus) or we are sent away from God (who says, **Depart from me. I never knew you)**. This is why Paul can say that when he dies, he has no qualms for he knows he will go to **be with the Lord. (Philippians 2:23)** This is based solely on faith in Christ.

So, when I die, and if St. Peter really is there, if there really is a gate, and he says to me, "Why should I let you into our heaven?" I'm not going to say because I preached my heart out every week for 50 years and I taught Sunday School and I went to seminary and all that. No, I'm just going to say, "Jesus, the Son of God, died on the cross for my sins and I have been forgiven. I don't deserve heaven, but he said he would save me a place, and I'm coming to claim my place." So the first judgment is at death when God says either "forgiven," or "depart from me."

But there yet remains a second, and final judgment pronounced at the end – the Great Day of Judgment, based upon our works. It doesn't affect the eternal destiny of the true believer in Christ, but for the believer has more to do with rewards. This is the culminating moment of all human history. Jesus said of his return in Matthew 16:17:

> **The Son of man is going to come with his angels in the glory of his father, and then he will repay each person according to what he has done.**

St. Paul described this in 2 Corinthians 5:1:

> **For we must all appear before the judgment seat of Christ, so that each one**

may receive what is due for what he has done in the body, whether good or evil.

St. John describes this in Revelation 20:11-13:

Then I saw a great white throne and the one who sat on it; the earth and the heaven fled from his presence, and no place was found for them. And I saw the dead, great and small, standing before the throne, and books were opened. Also another book was opened, the book of life. And the dead were judged according to their works, as recorded in the books. And the sea gave up the dead that were in it, Death and Hades gave up the dead that were in them, and all were judged according to what they had done.

This is the day the Apostle had in mind when he wrote these words in 1 Corinthians 3:13:

There is going to come a time of testing at the Judgment Day to see what kind of work each builder has done. Everyone's work will be put through the fire to see whether or not it keeps its value. If the work survives the fire, the builder will receive a reward. But if the work is burned up, the builder will suffer great loss. The builders themselves will be saved but like someone escaping through a wall of flames.

The efforts to which we give ourselves in this life, which have eternal significance, survive and bring us additional blessing and honor in heaven. You may not think this important, but God most assuredly does. He maintains a faithful record of all the faithful works of his people on earth, and it will be repeated aloud in heaven. Your acts of faithfulness and kindness that no one else knows except God are being carefully recorded. How many times have you reached out to help someone when you couldn't see a response? He keeps track right down to every cup of cold water we've given the needy in his name. (Mark 9:41) Oh, how embarrassing and devastating it would be not to have lived a life of kindness and faithfulness!

Whenever you make the effort to serve another human being God takes note – whatever the outcome. Whenever you change a diaper or do the dishes, whenever you stop by to check on your neighbor, when you encourage her, when you pray for him, when you give to the poor, when you stop and smile and show an interest in some lonely person, when you share about Christ with another, when you speak up for the rights of someone who is oppressed, when you work for the protection of the unborn.

In a sense, there are <u>two heavens</u>. First, there is heaven NOW, that invisible realm inhabited by God and his angels, where those faithful ones who have died are now. Second, there is heaven as it will BECOME, after the Final Judgment, when God ushers in the New Heaven and the New Earth. This may not be the most accurate way of describing this but it is a way I find helpful.

When the thief on the cross repented and believed in Christ, Jesus said to him, **Today you will be with me in Paradise. (Luke 23:43)**

When Paul was worn out and longing for heaven, he wrote his friends in Philippi, saying, **My desire is to depart and be with Christ. (Philippians 1:23)**

To the Corinthians he said he'd rather be at home with the Lord in heaven, even though it meant leaving his earthly body behind. (2 Corinthians 5:8)

When the believer dies, she leaves behind her body and enters into the next life to be with the Lord and all the others who have departed in faith. We're not talking about the Roman doctrine of purgatory – a place where we go to be purged of our sins prior to heaven. Great saints have disagreed about this but as I read the scripture, our sins are completely forgiven – here and now! The next life is "far better" according to St. Paul. But scripture teaches that this is not the end and it isn't nearly so good as it will be later on when God gives to us our new eternal bodies and we are permanently located on his New Earth.

Let me repeat this: When a lover of Christ dies, he goes into heaven but it is only an intermediate heaven there we will await the moment of Christ's return to earth, our bodily resurrection, the Final Judgment and the creation of the New Heaven and the New Earth.

Perhaps this seems odd to you but when you study scripture this is the conclusion to which you are driven. Maybe at first it seems strange to say the heaven we go to at death isn't eternal, yet it's true. Heaven as it NOW is, isn't complete, isn't finished. The biblical teaching is that there will be <u>New</u> Heaven and New Earth – an entirely renewed creation of God, a marvelous joining of heaven to earth where we will live with God.

Suppose you live in a trailer park in Maryland, and one day you inherit a marvelous home in Honolulu! Along with that, you are given a wonderful new job in Hawaii, doing what you've always longed to do, and many of your dearest loved ones will be living around you there. On your flight from DC to Honolulu you have a stopover in Seattle, where you'll spend an afternoon, and there you'll have a wonderful reunion with other dear family members you haven't seen in years.

Now, when you board the plane here in DC, and the ticket agent asks you where you're headed, you won't say Seattle – you'll just say, "I'm going to Hawaii!" You aren't likely even to mention to your friends that you'll be stopping over in Seattle because it's just a stop along the way. Your permanent home is Honolulu.

In the same way, the heaven we will go to when we die, the intermediate heaven, is a temporary stop along the way to our final destination, the New Earth. The illustration really isn't completely apt, because what really happens when we die is that the journey we take is more like a <u>round trip ticket</u>, because <u>in the end we'll return to earth</u> – but it will be wondrously changed as described in this vision of heaven from Revelation 21:1-5a:

> **Then I saw a new heaven and a new earth; for the first heaven and the first earth had passed away, and the sea was no more. And I saw the holy city, the new Jerusalem, coming down out of heaven from God, prepared as a bride adorned for her husband. And I heard a loud voice from the throne saying, "See, the home of God is among mortals. He will dwell with them; they will be his peoples, and God himself will be with them; he will wipe every tear from their eyes. Death will be no more; mourning and crying and pain will be no more, for the first things have passed away." And the one who was seated on the throne said, "See, I am making all things new."**

I think Anthony Hoekema, the theologian, is right when he writes:

> The "new Jerusalem"...does not remain in a 'heaven' far off in space, but it comes down to the renewed earth; there the redeemed will spend eternity in resurrection bodies. So heaven and earth, now separated, will then be merged: the new earth will also be heaven, since God will dwell there with his people. Glorified believers, in other words, will continue to be in heaven while they are inhabiting the new earth.

Or hear Michael Wittmer, who says in his book, <u>Heaven is a Place on Earth</u>:

> Our temporary stay in heaven – what theologians call the intermediate state – is not the primary focus of scripture. There are only a few verses that even allude to it. Scripture is relatively silent on our intermediate state in heaven because it is not the Christian hope. The Christian hope is not merely that our departed souls will rejoice in heaven, but that, as 1 Corinthians 15 explains, they will reunite with our resurrected bodies.
>
> And where do these bodies live? Bodies are meant to live on earth, on this planet. So the Christian hope is not merely that someday we and our loved ones will die and go to be with Jesus. Instead, the Christian hope is that our departure from this world is just the first leg of a journey that is round trip. We will not remain forever with God in heaven, for God will bring heaven down to us. As John explains his vision in Revelation 21: 1-4: **[He] saw the Holy City, the new Jerusalem, coming down out of heaven from God to earth,** accompanied by the thrilling words, **Now the dwelling of God is with men and he will live with them.**
>
> In short, Christians long for the fulfillment of Emmanuel, the divine name that means, "God with us." We don't hope merely for the day when we go to live with God, but ultimately for that final day when God comes to live with us.

Friends, we're talking about things that we really don't know all that much about. But, this first heaven, the intermediate heaven, may not be very far from us at all. It seems in some parts of scripture to be very near, a part of this universe but a part that we cannot see because of our spiritual blindness. In the gospel story of Christ's transfiguration, it describes Moses and Elijah suddenly appearing in bodily recognizable form from nowhere and dwelling on the mountaintop with Jesus and encouraging him and then departing. They simply appeared from heaven. When we die, it may not be so much that we go to a different universe as that we go to a larger, greater realm to which we've just been blind all along. Dallas Willard said, "When we pass through what we call death, we do not lose the world. Indeed, we see it for the first time as it really is."

Now some of you sharper Bible students will quote 2 Peter 3:10, which seems to say that in the end God will destroy the earth. "The heavens will disappear with a roar," the "elements one day will be destroyed by fire," and "the earth and everything in it will be laid bare." But this doesn't necessarily mean the earth will be annihilated. I like what John Piper says about this in his book, Future Grace: "What Peter may well mean is that at the end of this age there will be cataclysmic events that bring this world to an end as we know it – not putting it out of existence, but wiping out all that is evil and cleansing it by fire and fitting it for an age of glory and righteousness and peace that will never end."

This is not unlike what happened in the flood in Noah's time.

When John says in Revelation 21 that the first earth had passed away, perhaps he meant it in the sense that we would say the caterpillar is gone but now the butterfly emerges! One reason I believe this is that St. Paul tells us that this earth is longingly awaiting its rebirth. A day is coming that causes Paul to picture creation itself, standing on tiptoe, watching, waiting. Listen to Romans 8:19-22 (Petersen's The Message):

> **I don't think there's any comparison between the present hard times and the coming good times. The created world itself can hardly wait for what's coming next. Everything in creation is being more or less held back. God reins it in until both creation and all the creatures are ready and can be released at the same moment into the glorious times ahead. Meanwhile, the joyful anticipation deepens. All around us we observe a pregnant creation. The difficult times of pain throughout the world are simply birth pangs.**

Many honest people will tell me it troubles them that they really don't long for heaven all that much. Instead they love the earth but they find themselves longing for things here on earth to be the way God meant them to be in the first place before sin entered the world. This is exactly right. This is what heaven will be. To say to someone who is so fully alive to all the beauty of this world, "Well, you know, earth is not your home." That's like throwing cold water on a fire that we really should be fanning. Oh, there's much in this world that we tire of, that we hate – sin and pain and crime. We hate our own human stupidity sometimes, but there's so much that we love. We love the skyline of Washington, DC, and that mighty river that rolls by it. We love the spaciousness of the sky and the Blue Ridge in the glorious spring. We love barbeque on the grill under a warm summer night. I love sitting down with a good cup of coffee in the morning when no one else is up. I love getting into my car on a Sunday afternoon and turning on the Nationals and just driving off and listening to them play by play, or to Beethoven or Pavarotti, or even the Beatles! There's so much in this life that is so beautiful. There are so many things we love. This isn't heaven, but a foretaste. It's a preview of greater life to come.

Jesus, when he looked ahead to the end of time, said the earth is like a mother about to give birth to a new earth where God reigns in the midst of his people. (Matthew 24:7-8) He described what's coming as the <u>New</u> World – literally the "Regeneration." (Matthew 19:28) Surely this, too, is what the prophets saw as well – they saw a New Heaven and New Earth, in which·

> **The wolf also shall dwell with the lamb,**
> **and the leopard shall lie down with the kid;**

> **and the calf and the young lion and the fatling together, and a little child shall lead them. And the cow and the bear shall feed; their young ones shall lie down together. And the lion shall eat straw like the ox. And the nursing child shall play on the hole of the asp, and the weaned child shall put his hand on the adder's den. They shall not hurt nor destroy in all my holy mountain; for the earth shall be full of the knowledge of the Lord, as the waters cover the sea. (Isaiah 11:6-9; also 65:25; Numbers 14:21; Micah 4:3; Habakkuk 2:14)**

Friends, what does all this mean for us, now? When your heart is filled with a sense of wonder or appreciation, for the glory of a sunset, for the splendor of a huge tree canopied above, or when the sweetness of a child's smile captivates you, that is a little hint, an intimation of better, much better things to come. When you are hurting or disappointed, when your friends or your leaders let you down, or you fail yourself, that groaning within you is somehow in sync with the groaning of creation itself – these are birth pangs pointing to God's glorious future when there will be no more pain, no more sorrow! When you are tempted to withdraw or to hold back in doing the good that you can do and should do, tempted to give up, to quit – <u>Don't</u>. God is watching – nothing is wasted. Every good deed will be remembered in heaven.

What follows is a portion of a poem by John Piper in which he has been describing the great change which

God will bring about at the end, when the judgment is over and the New Earth begins.

> And as he spoke, the throne
> Of God came down to earth and shone
> Like golden crystal full of light,
> And banished, once for all, the night.
> And from the throne a stream began
> To flow and laugh, and as it ran,
> It made a river and a lake,
> And everywhere it flowed, a wake
> Of grass broke on the banks and spread
> Like resurrection from the dead.
>
> And in the twinkling of an eye
> The saints descended from the sky.
>
> And as I knelt beside the brook
> To drink eternal life, I took
> A glance across the golden grass,
> And saw my dog, old Blackie, fast
> As she could come. She leaped the stream –
> Almost – and what a happy gleam
> Was in her eye. I knelt to drink,
> And knew that I was on the brink
> Of endless joy. And everywhere
> I turned I saw a wonder there.
> A big man running on the lawn:
> That's old John Younge with both legs on.
> The blind can see a bird on wing,
> The dumb can lift their voice and sing.

The diabetic eats at will,
The coronary runs uphill.

The lame can walk, the deaf can hear.
The cancer-ridden bone is clear,
Arthritic joints are lithe and free,
And every pain has ceased to be.
And every sorrow deep within,
And every trace of lingering sin
Is gone. And all that's left is joy,
And endless ages to employ
The mind and heart, and understand.
And love the sovereign Lord who planned
That it should take eternity
To lavish all his grace on me.

O, God of wonder, God of might.
Grant us some elevated sight,
Of endless days. And let us see
The joy of what is yet to be.
And may your future make us free,
And guard us by the hope that we,
Through grace on lands that you restore,
Are justified for evermore.

Chapter 3

What Is Life Like In Heaven *Now*?

For the past several years I have been reading books about heaven – the oldest is titled, <u>The Saints Everlasting Rest</u>. It was published in 1650, written by Richard Baxter, a Puritan pastor. It is 672 pages of meditations on heaven! But after finishing it, I came away still wondering, "What is it LIKE in heaven?"

Most who have written about heaven say something like this: "We can't really know what it is like but it will be more wonderful than we can imagine! I don't personally find that particularly inspiring or helpful.

I've always loved the strong writings of Bishop J.C. Ryle of Liverpool who died in 1900. He said this:

> The man who is about to sail for Australia or New Zealand as a settler, is naturally anxious to know something about his future home, its climate, its employments, its inhabitants, its ways, its customs. All these are subjects of deep interest to him. You are leaving the land of your nativity, you are going to spend the rest of your life in a new hemisphere. It would be strange indeed if you did not desire information about your new abode. Now surely, if we hope to dwell forever in that 'better country, even a heavenly one,' we ought to seek all the knowledge we can get about it. Before we go to our eternal home we should try to become acquainted with it.

I have told you that there is more to be known about heaven, but the reason we know so little is we don't notice what the Bible says about heaven, and even when we do, we don't use our imagination.

Let's look at just two pieces of scripture – one a story Jesus told, and the second, a portion of a vision given to the Apostle John. We'll ask the question, "What does this tell us about heaven, now?"

We learned that, according to the Bible, at the very end of time, God will join heaven and earth into New Heaven and New Earth, but <u>for now</u>, those who die, who are true believers in Christ are with Him in what we describe as intermediate heaven – a sort of temporary stopover for believers until the final Resurrection and Judgment. And the moment when heaven comes down to the New Earth, our eternal home, is born.

Every time someone I love dies, it causes me to ponder afresh, what is life like for her <u>now</u>? Not what will life be like in heaven forever, but <u>now</u>, in this temporary state?

Read this story Jesus tells in Luke 16:19-31:

> There was a rich man who was dressed in purple and fine linen and who feasted sumptuously every day. And at his gate lay a poor man named Lazarus, covered with sores, who longed to satisfy his hunger with what fell from the rich man's table; even the dogs would come and lick his sores. The poor man died and was carried away by the angels to be with Abraham.* The rich man also died and was buried. In Hades, where he was being tormented, he looked up and saw Abraham far away with Lazarus by his side.* He called out, "Father Abraham, have mercy on me, and send Lazarus to dip the tip of his finger in water and cool my tongue; for I am in agony in these flames." But Abraham said, "Child, remember that during your lifetime you received your good things, and Lazarus in like manner evil things; but now he is comforted here, and you are in agony. Besides all this, between you and us a great chasm has been fixed, so that those who might want to pass from here to you cannot do so, and no one can cross from there to us." He said, "Then, father, I beg you to send him to my father's house – for I have five brothers – that he may warn them, so that they will not also come into this place of torment." Abraham replied, "They have

> Moses and the prophets; they should listen to them." He said, "No, father Abraham; but if someone goes to them from the dead, they will repent." He said to him, "If they do not listen to Moses and the prophets, neither will they be convinced even if someone rises from the dead."

I remember in graduate school reading a learned commentary on this parable in which the author said, "Of course, we are not to infer anything about the actual <u>condition</u> in the next life from this parable – surely it is all figurative language." Now, reading it years later, I'm not so sure about that.

My guess is that we shouldn't insist that every detail is to be taken literally, but at the same time, I think surely the Lord intended that we understand that in the next life, people are still real human beings, with thoughts and concerns; the same identity as here in this life, with clear memory of life on earth, and at least somehow aware of things going on still on earth. He certainly wants us to know that heaven and hell are real places where there are real people.

Let's just note the major points of the story.

The main character is named Lazarus – in all the stories Jesus told which are recorded in the New Testament, this is the only one where a person is actually named – it may be Jesus was speaking of a real man, known to his hearers. His name, "Lazarus," means "God helps." The story may indeed be about two real people.

When Lazarus dies, the angels carry him to Paradise. The rich man died and went to a place of torment – Hades. It's a shadowy word, meaning darkness or "the pit." Lazarus is with Abraham – our father in faith, and by inference with others close to God, the rich man seems to be alone.

Paradise – or the intermediate heaven – and Hades are separated by a fixed chasm. But here, they can see each other at least in some limited way.

Both Lazarus and the rich man ("Dives" – he is called by later generations) reason and communicate. There is a direct continuity between their earthly lives and afterlives.

Each is pictured as having a body. The rich man speaks of his tongue and being thirsty. He swallows physically. Lazarus has water to drink and a finger to dip into the water.

The rich man has clear recall of his brothers still on earth – he may even see them. He is concerned for his lost brothers.

Abraham says none can cross the chasm between heaven and hell.

C.S. Lewis said:

> All your life an unattainable ecstasy has hovered just beyond the grasp of your consciousness. The day is coming when you will wake to find, beyond all hope, that you have attained it, or else, that it was within your reach and you have lost it forever.

Now <u>if</u> these basic teachings are consistent with other teachings in other parts of the Bible, then a strong case can be made that these principles we've observed are more than just symbolic.

Let's look at just one other passage – only a portion of chapter 6 of the Revelation of John. In fact, just three verses. This vision is a part of a much larger section in which the apostle is given a vision of coming events, similar to the visions Daniel and Ezekiel received. Most of the rest of the Revelation is actually various scenes from heaven – either how things are <u>now</u> in heaven or things yet to be.

This is apocalyptic literature, which by definition is usually sensational and dramatic and mysterious. Many would say this is simply the record of one religious man's wild, exaggerated imagination. But in the church, we take all the scriptures very seriously – it is <u>all</u> the Word of God.

Here in Revelation 6 is a snapshot of a moment in the intermediate heaven – again, perhaps not to be taken completely literally, but just observe with me for a moment. Here is what it says in vv. 9-11:

> **When he opened the fifth seal, I saw under the altar the souls of those who had been slaughtered for the word of God and for the testimony they had given; they cried out with a loud voice, 'Sovereign Lord, holy and true, how long will it be before you judge and avenge our blood on the inhabitants of the earth?' They were each**

> **given a white robe and told to rest a little longer, until the number would be complete both of their fellow-servants and of their brothers and sisters, who were soon to be killed as they themselves had been killed.**

First he describes people who have died – now they are in heaven. While on earth they were martyred for their faith in Christ. There is a direct continuity between one's earthly identity and identity in heaven. These are the same people they were on earth. They've just been relocated. People in the next life are remembered by the lives they lived on earth.

Next, notice that in heaven they speak audibly. They have mouths and voices and vocal equipment and can <u>raise</u> their voice. So they are emotional, rational communicators. Here they are pictured as full of passion, and they speak in a unified voice – heaven is a place of unity and shared perspectives. They are rational and aware of each other and of things on earth. They ask God to intervene on earth and act on their behalf.

Those who are in heaven now – right now, are evidently close to God, free to ask him questions to pray on behalf of those on earth. They ask God, "How long before you judge those on earth who do evil?" So they have a desire to learn, to understand. They know what's happening on earth, they have a great longing to see justice done on earth, to see evil ended and punished.

Those who are now in heaven are not passive and

disinterested in what's happening here. Their concerns for righteousness and justice may even be greater in heaven. They clearly remember their lives on earth: these remembered that they had been murdered, and as they pray for judgment on their persecutors who are still persecuting, it implies they are interceding for the suffering saints in earth.

Notice how they address God as "Sovereign," "Holy and True." In heaven they see more clearly what God is like and perhaps this causes them to understand more clearly the seriousness of sin.

In heaven, people are distinct individuals – each is given his <u>own</u> robe. This seems to say also they have bodies – disembodied spirits don't wear clothing! Maybe the robes are symbolic but that doesn't mean they aren't physical – John sees people, individuals in this vision.

God answers their questions which demonstrates that we certainly won't <u>know everything</u> in heaven, and we will continue to learn.

God says they must wait awhile longer, so those in heaven now are living in anticipation of God's future fulfillment of his promise. Now notice there is <u>time</u> in the next life. They ask how long will it be. They are eager for the time of judgment to finally arrive. God says they must wait a little longer.

Note the sense of <u>closeness</u> between those in heaven now and those they love on earth whom they call "fellow servants and brothers" (brothers and sisters). We who belong to Christ are one family with those who have gone before us.

Then last, notice that God knows every detail of what is happening on earth and what <u>will</u> happen, right down to every drop of blood shed by his children who are being persecuted for their faith here on earth.

A few years ago, "Voice of the Martyrs," an international watchdog group, estimated more than 150,000 people die each year because of their faith in Christ. That's more than 400 a day – God knows the names, the circumstances of every one. He knows how many will die and he is ready to return and set up his kingdom when that number is complete and the last one has been martyred

I'm grateful to my friend Randy Alcorn for helping me to see all of this in these three brief verses. The point I want to make is just this – I don't see any reason, really, to suppose that these observations apply just to the one group John saw but to no one else in heaven. I believe what was true for them is true for all those who are now with the Lord, and will be true for us when we die, if we are faithful to Christ.

Think of a faithful brother or sister or mother or father in Christ, now deceased:

- Is that person still <u>the same</u> <u>individual</u>? Yes.
- Is that person <u>in a</u> real <u>place</u>? Yes.
- Does he or she have <u>a real body</u>? We can't say positively, but it appears that God grants us some

kind of body, even though it's not our final, perfected resurrected body. In this life, we do not exist without a body – there is a direct and intimate relationship between the body and the spirit – we aren't spirits who inhabit bodies – we are human beings; with both a spirit and a body – that' what a person is!

When Paul wrote of his amazing experiences of being caught up into the intermediate heaven, he said he really wasn't certain whether he'd had a body or not (2 Corinthians 12:3), **"Whether in the body or apart from the body, I do not know, but God knows."** Maybe it doesn't matter much, but remember that Christ's resurrected body was physical but not limited, as ours are now. So he at least has a body and it appears others in the intermediate heaven do also, although they are only temporary.

Do people in heaven now <u>see what is happening on earth</u>? Over and over, the little snapshots of heaven the Bible allows us to glimpse, imply the answer is absolutely yes – when Samuel came back from the dead before Saul, Samuel well knew what was happening to Saul. When Moses and Elijah came from heaven to meet with Jesus on the Mount of Transfiguration, they seemed fully aware of all that was going on.

Hebrews 12:1 lays out an image of all the believers in heaven surrounding, watching, encouraging us from afar to persevere and to be faithful.

Therefore, since we are surrounded by so great a cloud of witnesses, let us also lay aside every weight and the sin that clings so closely, and let us run with perseverance the race that is set before us.

This is what we mean by "the Communion of the Saints."

Sometime ago I told a story about baseball in heaven, which elicited an unexpected, wonderful story from one of our church families – one of our ladies – a dear friend who wrote the following.

> Today when you were talking about the possibility that there may be baseball in heaven, I was reminded of something that happened shortly after my brother-in-law died twelve years ago.
>
> Jerry Bosse was a natural athlete who particularly loved baseball. Following high school graduation, he was drafted by the Mets as a left-handed first baseman. Due to his height of 5'11", they told him he would never make the majors, so his professional career was cut short after 2 years. Nevertheless, he continued playing as a semi-pro and a recreational player, was an avid Orioles fan, and coached for his children's baseball teams even after a botched back surgery left him partially paralyzed.
>
> A month after his 53rd birthday, he awoke telling my sister he thought he was having a

heart attack. Two hours later he was with the Lord. Our entire family was devastated, and his 21 year old son was particularly bereft. Because of an earlier discussion with Jerry, my sister had his ashes spread over the infield at Camden Yards. This happened at 6 am one Sunday morning because one of Jerry's good friends was the grounds keeper at the stadium and let them in to fulfill this wish of Jerry's.

My nephew had caught baseball fever from his dad, mostly as a spectator. He had season tickets to see the Orioles. The day my brother-in-law should have turned 54, his son was in his seat at the Orioles game, of course missing his father and remembering their many times watching baseball together. Before he knew what was happening, a home run was hit right to him. He came home from the game telling my sister what happened and saying, "I think Dad must have been watching the game on his birthday from heaven." Needless to say, they were blessed, and my nephew who had felt so alone without his dad, realized though out of sight, his dad was still there and still cared.

The following year, again on Jerry's birthday, his son had tickets to the Orioles. He was a bit late arriving at his seat so when he arrived, his buddy said, "You should have been here, Jerry. A home run was hit to your seat." He showed young Jerry the caught ball. Jerry sat down, and within a half hour, a second home run was hit, this time directly to him. That night, he again came home showing my sister the two caught balls and saying, "Dad must have been there again…it was too much of a coincidence…two years in a row on his birthday." He again, was incredibly blessed.

So, maybe if there isn't baseball in heaven, perhaps those in heaven can watch the games here. Either way, God was really wonderful to show my bereaved nephew that He was with him and his father was with him even though he was in heaven…through baseball.

Do people in heaven pray for those on earth? If we are closer to God in heaven, and if prayer is simply talking to God, then presumably we'd pray much <u>more</u>. Christ is described as now interceding for people on earth (Romans 8:34; 1 John 2:1), and asking God to take specific action for the sake of his children on earth.

If people in heaven are allowed to see at least some of what is transpiring here on earth, wouldn't it seem strange if they <u>didn't</u> pray for us? They share our concerns in <u>some</u> way, I expect.

In the end, in the final heaven that scripture describes as New Heaven – New Earth, the word says that God will take away all grief, all sorrow (Revelation 21:4).

But that is yet to be. For now, I believe those who are <u>with Christ, share his concerns and his compassion for all who are still in this life, and in need or in trouble</u>.

But this shouldn't discourage us. Paul says that though it's right and normal to grieve when someone we love dies, we are not to grieve like those who have no hope (1 Thessalonians 4:13) or worry about them. Though they share in some way still, in the sadnesses of earth, at the same time now they are experiencing the joy of Christ in a place so wonderful it's called Paradise.

One day, Paul says, those of us here who are faithful to Christ will be joined again with those we love who have died, and there will be a glorious reunion and "we will be with the Lord forever. Therefore, says scripture, **"encourage each other with these words." (1 Thessalonians 4:13)**

Should we pray for our loved ones now in heaven? Well, it just seems so natural – I'm sure it's appropriate, even though how to pray for someone who's in Paradise and has all he could need, is another question. I content myself with thanking God for them, that they are with Him, and praying they'll know I love them.

I don't know what your life is like – I know that sometimes in my life I succumb to discouragement, sometimes I'm just exhausted and ready to give up. But I am learning to keep the end in sight, to keep heaven always before me, and it gives me great, great hope.

In 1952, young Florence Chadwick stepped into the waters of the Pacific Ocean off Catalina Island, determined to swim to the shore of mainland California. She'd already been the first woman to swim the English Channel both ways. The weather was foggy and chilly; she could hardly see the boats accompanying her. Still she swam for fifteen hours. When she begged to be taken out of the water along the way, her mother, in a boat alongside, told her she was close and that she could make it. Finally, physically and emotionally exhausted, she stopped swimming and was pulled out. It wasn't until she was on the boat that she discovered the shore was less than half a mile away. At a news conference the next day she said, "All I could see was the fog...I think if I could have seen the shore, I would have made it."

For believers, the shore is heaven – Jesus is standing there, very close to us, though hidden from our sight. He is saying, and his words are echoed by countless other voices:

> Carry on, dear friend – you can do it
> No matter how difficult the challenge...
> I am with you
> I will not fail you
> I will see you through . . . forever!

And so we close with these powerful and encouraging words about Jesus:

> **Now to him who is able to keep you from stumbling and to present you blameless before the presence of his glory with great joy, to the only God, our Savior, through Jesus Christ our Lord, be glory, majesty, dominion and authority, before all time and now and forever. Amen. (Jude 24-25)**

Made in the USA
Columbia, SC
06 January 2025